D1558323

KILLER ANIMALS
CROCODILES
ON THE HUNT

by Lori Polydoros

Reading Consultant:
Barbara J. Fox
Reading Specialist
North Carolina State University

Content Consultants:
Joe Maierhauser, President/CEO
Terry Phillip, Curator of Reptiles
Reptile Gardens
Rapid City, South Dakota

Capstone
press

Mankato, Minnesota

Blazers is published by Capstone Press,
151 Good Counsel Drive, P.O. Box 669, Mankato, Minnesota 56002.
www.capstonepress.com

Library of Congress Cataloging-in-Publication Data
Polydoros, Lori, 1968–
    Crocodiles: on the hunt/by Lori Polydoros.
    p. cm. — (Blazers. Killer animals)
    Includes bibliographical references and index.
    Summary: "Describes crocodiles, their physical features, how they hunt and kill, and their
role in the ecosystem" — Provided by publisher.
    ISBN-13: 978-1-4296-2314-8 (hardcover)
    ISBN-10: 1-4296-2314-4 (hardcover)
    1. Crocodiles — Juvenile literature. I. Title.
QL666.C925P65 2009
597.98'2 — dc22
                                                          2008029853

Editorial Credits
Abby Czeskleba, editor; Kyle Grenz, designer; Wanda Winch, photo researcher

Photo Credits
Ardea/M. Watson, 14–15
Art Life Images/age fotostock/Fritz Poelking, 16; Horizon Stock Images/Gloria Cotton, 24–25;
    Morales, 11; Werner Bollmann, 12–13, 18–19
Creatas, cover
DigitalVision, 4–5
Getty Images Inc./De Agostini Picture Library/DEA/C. Dani — I. Jeske, 8–9
Minden Pictures/Suzi Eszterhas, 20–21
Nature Picture Library/Anup Shah, 6–7, 22–23
Peter Arnold/Biosphoto/Gunther Michel, 13 (inset); Tim Rock, 28–29
Shutterstock/Emilia Stasiak, 26–27

1 2 3 4 5 6 14 13 12 11 10 09

TABLE OF CONTENTS

UNDERWATER SPY

A crocodile swims underwater as a wildebeest walks nearby. The crocodile's eyes and **nostrils** peek above the water's surface. The crocodile waits for the right time to attack.

nostril – an opening in an animal's nose used for breathing

5

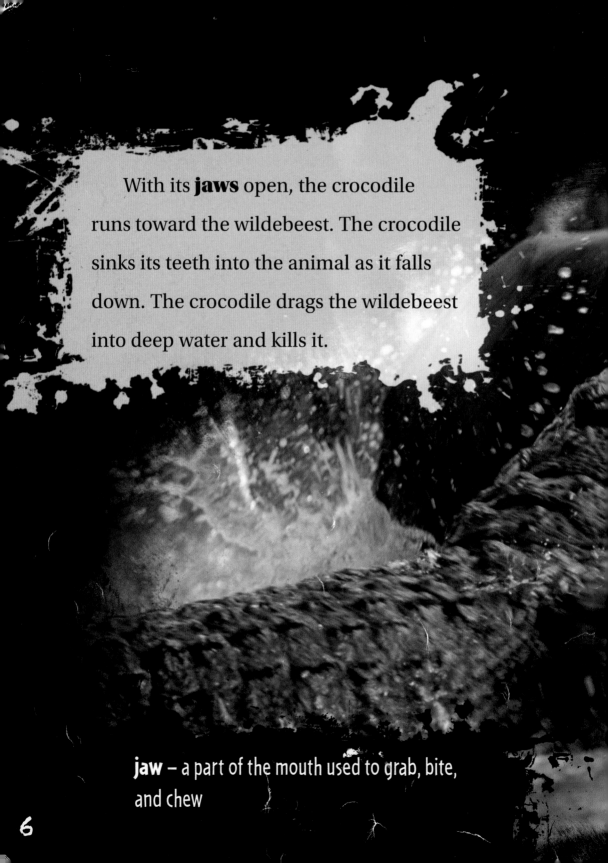

With its **jaws** open, the crocodile runs toward the wildebeest. The crocodile sinks its teeth into the animal as it falls down. The crocodile drags the wildebeest into deep water and kills it.

jaw – a part of the mouth used to grab, bite, and chew

7

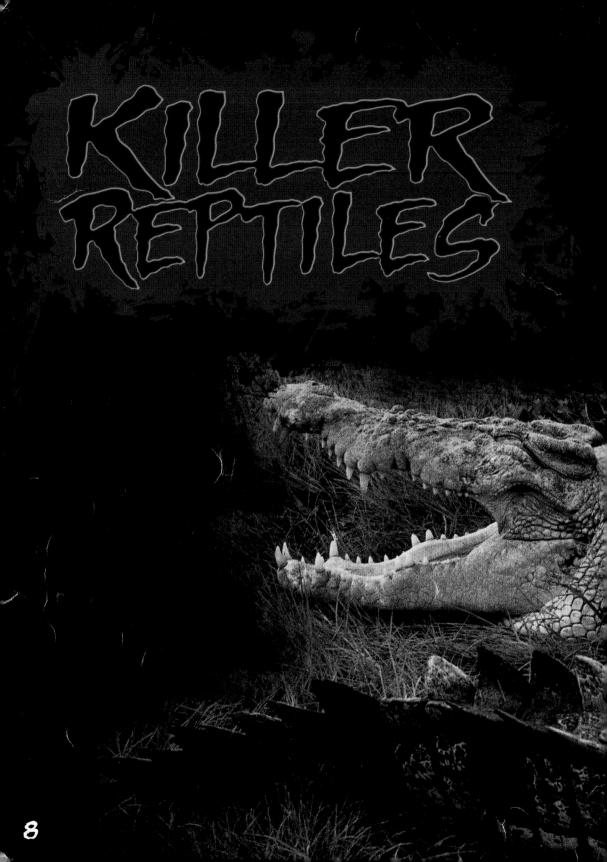

KILLER REPTILES

Crocodiles are some of the largest **reptiles** in the world. Most crocodiles grow to be as long as a car. They can weigh up to 2,000 pounds (907 kilograms).

reptile – a scaly-skinned animal that has the same body temperature as its surroundings

Crocodiles use their long tails to glide through water. Their tails also help them attack **prey** at lightning-fast speeds.

prey – an animal hunted by another animal

Crocodiles have sharp, pointy teeth. Their teeth help them strip the meat from prey. The strong teeth also break the bones of prey.

KILLER FACT

Crocodiles have 30 to 40 teeth in each jaw.

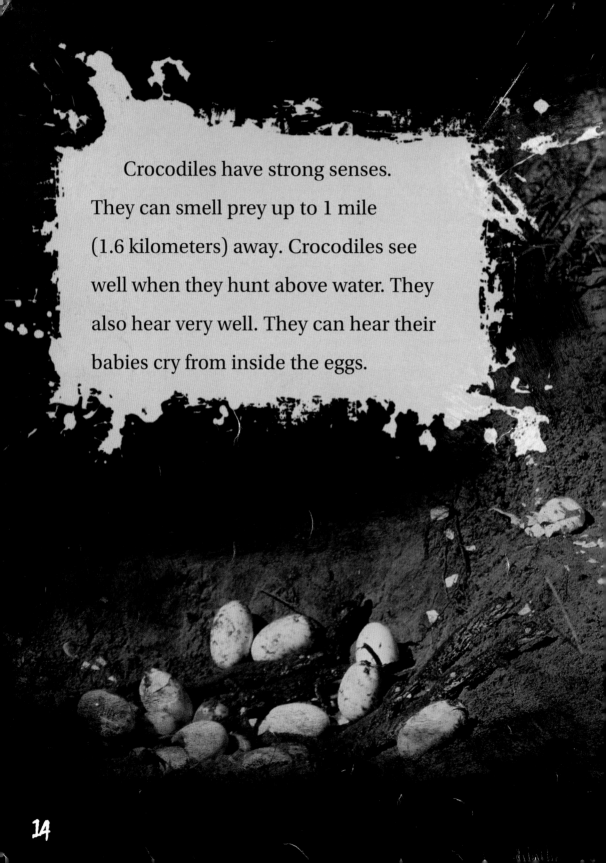

Crocodiles have strong senses. They can smell prey up to 1 mile (1.6 kilometers) away. Crocodiles see well when they hunt above water. They also hear very well. They can hear their babies cry from inside the eggs.

KILLER FACT

A crocodile's ears are hidden inside flaps.
These flaps are on the sides of its head.
The flaps close underwater.

MAKING THE KILL

Crocodiles **stalk** their prey on land and in water. On land, they blend in with their surroundings. They lie still for hours until an animal comes too close. Crocodiles also swim underwater to sneak up on prey.

stalk – to hunt an animal in a quiet, secret way

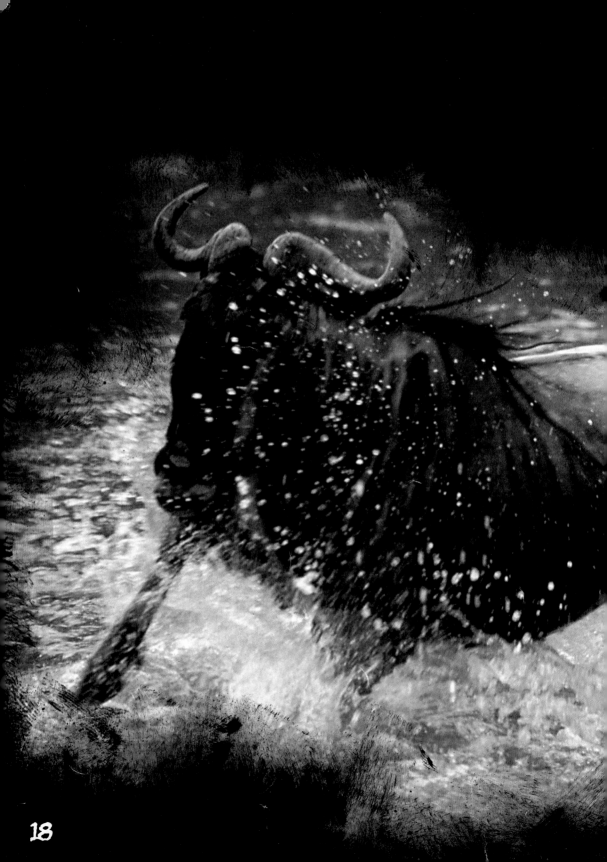

Crocodiles rush toward prey to attack. Some crocodiles can run up to 10 miles (16 kilometers) per hour. Crocodiles use their sharp teeth to grab prey.

Crocodiles drag their prey into deep water. The deep water makes it hard for prey to escape. Crocodiles drown an animal before eating it.

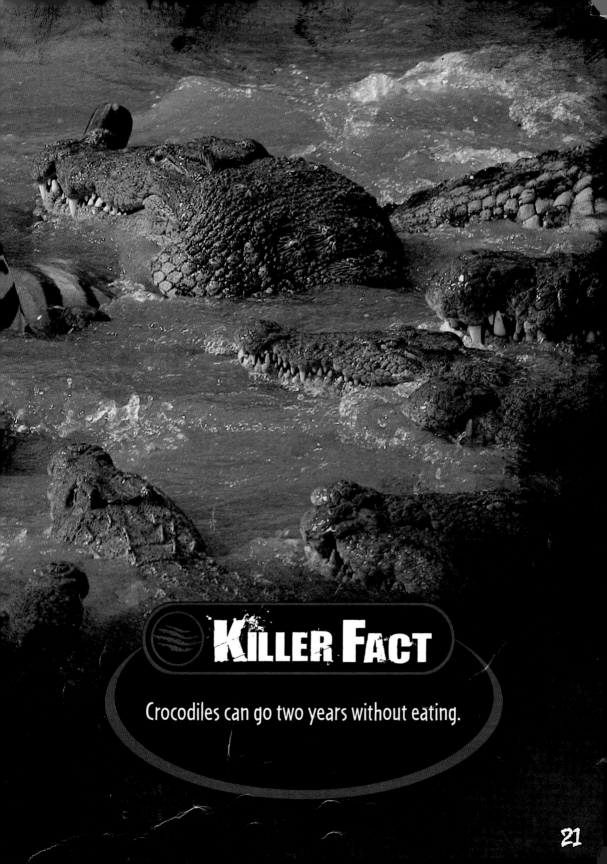

KILLER FACT

Crocodiles can go two years without eating.

Crocodile Diagram

scaly skin

eye

sharp tooth

HELPING THE ECOSYSTEM

Crocodiles play an important role in the **ecosystem**. They eat all kinds of prey. Without crocodiles, there would be too many animals of one kind. Too many animals can be bad for the ecosystem.

ecosystem – a group of animals and plants that work together with their surroundings

KILLER FACT

Some people kill crocodiles for their skin.
In the United States, it is against the law to
kill crocodiles.

Crocodiles may seem scary, but they rarely attack humans. We must protect these beasts in order for them to **survive**.

survive – to continue to live

Waiting to Attack!

GLOSSARY

ecosystem (EE-koh-sis-tuhm) — a group of animals and plants that work together with their surroundings

jaw (JAW) — a part of the mouth used to grab, bite, and chew

nostril (NOSS-truhl) — an opening in an animal's nose used for breathing

prey (PRAY) — an animal hunted by another animal for food

protect (pruh-TECT) — to keep something safe from harm or injury

reptile (REP-tile) — a scaly-skinned animal that has the same body temperature as its surroundings

stalk (STAWK) — to hunt an animal in a quiet, secret way

survive (sur-VIVE) — to continue to live

READ MORE

Kaufman, Gabriel. *Saltwater Crocodile: The World's Biggest Reptile.* SuperSized! New York: Bearport, 2007.

Landau, Elaine. *Alligators and Crocodiles: Hunters of the Night.* Animals After Dark. Berkeley Heights, N.J.: Enslow, 2008.

Thomas, Isabel. *Alligator vs. Crocodile.* Animals Head to Head. Chicago: Raintree, 2006.

INTERNET SITES

FactHound offers a safe, fun way to find educator-approved Internet sites related to this book.

Here's what you do:

1. Visit *www.facthound.com*
2. Choose your grade level.
3. Begin your search.

This book's ID number is 9781429623148.

FactHound will fetch the best sites for you!

INDEX